From Damaged to Destined

My Journey from Cult Member to Christian Leader

From Damaged to Destined

My Journey from Cult Member to Christian Leader

DR. KAREN HUTCHINS

LKM·publishing

LKM Publishing
516 Jefferic Blvd.
Dover, DE 19901
www.drkarenhutchins.com
Phone: 302-399-5169

©2018 Karen Hutchins

All rights reserved. No portion of this book may be reproduced, stored in a retrieval system, or transmitted in any form or by any means-electronic, mechanical, photocopy, recording, scanning, or other-except for brief quotation in critical reviews or articles, without the prior written permission of the publisher.

First Edition: December 2018

Scripture quotations marked (NIV) are taken from the Holy Bible, New International Version®, NIV®. Copyright © 1973, 1978, 1984, 2011 by Biblica, Inc.™ Used by permission of Zondervan. All rights reserved worldwide. www.zondervan.com The "NIV" and "New International Version" are trademarks registered in the United States Patent and Trademark Office by Biblica, Inc.™

All Scripture quotations, unless otherwise indicated, are taken from the (KJV) King James Version (Public Domain).

Scripture quotations marked CSB®, are taken from the Christian Standard Bible®, Copyright © 2017 by Holman Bible Publishers. Used by permission. Christian Standard Bible®, and CSB® are federally registered trademarks of Holman Bible Publishers.

Scripture quotations marked (AMP) are taken from the Amplified Bible, Copyright © 1954, 1958, 1962, 1964, 1965, 1987 by The Lockman Foundation. Used by permission.

Scripture quotations marked MSG are taken from THE MESSAGE, copyright © 1993, 1994, 1995, 1996, 2000, 2001, 2002 by Eugene H. Peterson. Used by permission of NavPress. All rights reserved. Represented by Tyndale House Publishers, Inc.

Scripture quotations are from The ESV® Bible (The Holy Bible, English Standard Version®), copyright © 2001 by Crossway, a publishing ministry of Good News Publishers. Used by permission. All rights reserved

Scripture quotations marked "ASV" are taken from the American Standard Version Bible (Public Domain).

Scripture quotations marked (TLB) are taken from The Living Bible copyright © 1971. Used by permission of Tyndale House Publishers, Inc., Carol Stream, Illinois 60188. All rights reserved.

ISBN-13: 978-0-578-42679-2

Printed in the United States of America

Contents

Dedication xi
Foreword xiii
Introduction xvii

   1. Life Before Christ 1
      Reflection 6
   2. Wolves in Sheep's Clothing 8
      Reflection 13
   3. The Journey to Awareness 15
      Reflection 20
   4. New Beginnings 22
      Reflection 28
   5. God's Mandated Assignment 30
      Reflection 34
   6. Destined by God 36
   7. Walking in Destiny 39

Acknowledgment 45

Dedication

This book is dedicated first and foremost, to my Lord and Savior, Jesus Christ, who is the reason for my existence.
To my loving and supportive husband, Bishop Norman Hutchins - words cannot express my sincere gratitude for the many late nights you stayed up with me as I penned this book.
To my son Sheldon, who gave me a reason to live for someone more than just myself.

Finally, to anyone who is in pursuit of Christ and has been misled in some way, be encouraged and know that "He which has begun a good work in you will perform it until the day of the Lord Jesus Christ." (Philippians 1:6)

Foreword

As I reflect on the state of our nation, my heart is burdened by the number of hurting people. Knowing that we are living in the 21st century, in a world flooded with distress, it's obvious that "no one" escapes the vicissitudes of life. As we journey through Dr. Karen Hutchins book you will read about many challenges in life. I am so proud of her for her first printed book: From Damaged to Destined. I am sure we all can relate to an experience or situation where we felt "damaged". Have you ever traveled to a destination and along the way experienced a flat tire? During the experience we don't flatten the other three tires, we challenge or correct the one flattened or damaged as there is nothing wrong with the vehicle. The issue is with that which is attached to the vehicle.

As you journey through this excellent read, allow this powerful book to compel you. Dr. Hutchins' transparency about her life experiences will speak to your heart. She takes us through being dented, bruised, upset, angry, bitter, as well as a period in her life of being disconnected from her family. She didn't allow her challenges and hardship to cause her to flat-line. Instead, she picked up the pieces and dealt with it head-on. There is a treasure in this earthen vessel. Reflect on your journey and dare not to give up due to setbacks in life. Walk in

Foreword

your God given mandate of purpose and know that our latter is far greater than our past. God is the Potter, we are the clay just know that He specializes in difficult situations. While many may have been "damaged" in life we are certain by the grace of God to be "Damaged Goods".

Dr. Carrie Carter

It was a lovely Saturday in May 2015 when I attended the Frontline Ministries Mother's Day program held at St Andrew's Church Fellowship Church in Dover, Delaware. It was a memorable event filled with wonderful tributes to the many mothers who were attending that day. The First Lady of Frontline Ministries, Karen Hutchins, was busy scurrying around making sure everyone and everything was in place for this tribute to all our mothers. Whether they were first-time mothers, mothers to be, mothers of many or few, grandmothers and great-grandmothers. Each mother was treated to a special recognition of their loving care and sacrifice as mothers.

My daughter, who participated in the beautiful dance ministries tribute to the mothers came to sit with me during the luncheon meal. Her first question," Mom, did you enjoy the performance?" I replied, "I did, it was wonderful." Then she said, "Did you get to speak with Lady Karen?" "No, she is really busy, and I did not want to interrupt." Well, Mom, she said all knowingly, you have to speak to her before we leave." I thought to myself, I doubt very seriously I will do that.

Anyone who knows me can tell you that I am very outgoing and friendly person, but I do not go out of my way to make my presence known in those situations. Usually, I quietly leave without a word to those who are hosting or to the guest of honor at the event. However, it so happened this time I stayed to help with the breaking down of the table cloths and decorations. As we were getting ready to leave the venue, Lady Karen greeted us and thanked me for coming. She grabbed my hand and placed some money into the palm of my hand. Happy Mother's Day she said, I looked at that money with disbelief, it was a $100-dollar bill. I was speechless!

Since becoming a Christian, at that time would have been for over thirty-six years, I had never received a monetary gift of any size from anyone at any of the churches I attended. So, you could imagine I was completely caught off guard with her kind gesture. For the most part, I have been the giver – of my time and resources serving in many roles. I never looked for any compensation; it was just an honor to serve the Lord and His people. Needless to say, her thoughtful gift brought tears to my eyes along with the realization that God is still using His servants to bless and meet the needs of His people. In 1 Thessalonians 5: 12-13, the scripture states

"Dear brothers and sisters, honor those who are your leaders in the Lord's work. They work hard among you and give you spiritual guidance. 13 Show them great respect and wholehearted love because of their work. And live peacefully with each other. New International Version (NIV)

At that moment, I had a sincere appreciation for those who are called to and work in the ministry of Jesus Christ. As

Foreword

a relatively new member of Frontline, I knew Karen Hutchins knew nothing about me. My own life story had an unconventional and tenuous beginning, living in a dysfunctional household growing up in a working-class neighborhood in Queens, NY. My life reflected the inner *"damaged goods"* that many of us have experienced. Our outside appearances may reflect the earthly successes - having a family, a spouse, children, a great career, friends, nice house, money to buy what we need, accolades from those around us. But on the inside, we have damaged areas that are in need of healing and restoration.

"From Damaged to Destined" was written by a woman who has the heart of a servant. She has experienced how it feels to be *damaged goods* but has learned to overcome by her faith and trust in the Lord Jesus Christ. She possesses the sensitivity to hear the voice of Lord and walk in His ways as she lives out her purpose in the Kingdom of God. I have witnessed her strength during times of significant trials and personal issues. Yet even in those times, she would demonstrate the love of Jesus Christ not only in word but in action. This book will encourage those of us who think we are invisible in the world, and who believe we are so "damaged" that we are of no real use to anyone. It is my hope that you will gain strength and peace as you read and enjoy *From Damaged to Destined*.

Dr. Phyllis Brooks-Collins

Introduction

Walmart is absolutely one of my favorite places! I can spend hours browsing casually along the aisles, finding bargains, checking out new seasonal items and of course, saving on groceries and essentials. One day, I was doing one of my many weekly Walmart visits along with my husband, and we happened to notice the cart of a woman who had piled up a huge number of large cans of green beans in her shopping cart.

"Okay," I thought, "she must be planning for a large event." But, upon closer inspection, I noticed that the cans were all damaged in some way or another. Some were dented, others had ripped or stained labels or were completely missing labels. As I watched the woman move toward the check-out area, I heard another shopper inquire, "Excuse me, but where did you get all those cans of green beans? And, are they on sale?" The woman smiled and responded cheerfully, "Oh, Yes! You can find all kinds of sale items in the back of the store. Look for the bin with the big sign "Damaged Goods."

"Wow! What a life-transforming illustration!" I thought. Many of us have been through the scratches and dents of life and been regarded as inadequate. We've been made to feel disqualified from the front of the line and pushed to the back, or worse, tossed aside as unworthy. Because of

Introduction

circumstances and situations, our value has been reduced in the eyes of others. We have been treated (or mistreated) and looked down upon.

The truth is, God's plan and purpose for our lives is still available to each of us. We all have been damaged but God is standing by to restore and revive us. As you read this book, you will be able to move from broken to whole, from hurt to healed, and from insecure to confident. If you are willing to put your trust in God, He will finish what He started! You will no longer feel damaged but will find hope and renewal in the God of your salvation.

Chapter 1

Life Before Christ

In February of 1967, I made my arrival into this world. My parents were from Belize, where the Roman Catholic religion is prevalent. Like most parents, my mom and dad concerned themselves with the physical, emotional and spiritual well-being of all their children. I had a pretty normal childhood, and our family attended a Catholic church. We believed in the life, death and resurrection of Jesus Christ, but we were also taught that the Pope was God's earthly ambassador.

It wasn't until I was about 24 that I was introduced to Pentecostalism. This was a seismic shift in my theology. Instead of stoic services filled with symbolism and rituals, I embraced a culture that emphasized the person, presence and work of the Holy Spirit in each believer's life. I became passionate about my newfound faith and threw myself into the work of ministry.

Ironically, before I got deeply involved in this ministry I was on the track of success. I completed college and got a great job that afforded a comfortable lifestyle. I was working as an administrative secretary for a tax service in Los Angeles. I had a nice home and car, good friends and a good husband, although he wasn't saved. Somehow, I knew spiritual life was lacking. So, when my brother and other friends would talk about Christ, and give all these glowing testimonies, it sparked something in me that made me want to pursue this relationship of grace and mercy.

I didn't know if all the testimonies were true, but I definitely wanted to learn more. I began reading the Bible and different Christian literature to gain more understanding. It was as if there was something drawing me in. I'd read for hours in the evenings and even during my lunch break at work. Finally, I came to a point where I told God, "If You're real, and You do all these things people say, prove Yourself to me and I'll serve you for the rest of my life." I was willing to reject all that I'd learned in my Catholic upbringing and commit myself to the Father, Son and Holy Spirit, but only if this 'Christianity' was going to be better.

I shared my quest for more spiritual knowledge with one of my sisters, and she connected me with one of her Christian friends. I had a lot of questions: *How do I know when God is speaking? Does God really answer our prayers? How do I acquire the Holy Ghost?* My sister's friend met me at a Chinese restaurant after work one evening. I timidly shared how I was feeling, but after our conversation, I felt ecstatic about the next steps on my spiritual journey.

A few days later, the friend invited me to visit a Christian service being hosted at a private home. As I prepared to leave for the service, the song "Take Me Back" (by Andre Crouch) echoed in my head.

Take me back, take me back dear Lord
To the place where I first received you

Life Before Christ

Take me back, take me back dear Lord where I
First believed
I feel that I'm so far from you Lord
But still I hear you calling me
Those simple things that I once knew
Their memories keep drawing me
I must confess, Lord I've been blessed
But yet my soul's not satisfied
Renew my faith, restore my joy
And dry my weeping eyes

When my son and I got to the house for the service, we were warmly welcomed. The service began, and the people joined together in the singing and clapping. It was wonderful! I'd never encountered a female pastor before, but this woman preached a powerful message and to my surprise, she closed out her sermon with the song "Take Me Back." Tears rolled down my cheeks as she sang. It was confirmation to me that I was in the right place and this was the right thing. Although my husband wasn't interested in attending church, he didn't stop me from going and taking our son. Eight weeks later, my son and I joined the ministry.

Involvement in ministry is interesting. In my mind, I was prepared for a glorious experience with Godly people who had synonymous goals and mindsets. I was in the midst of people, many of whom were contentious and exhibited some of the worst behavior imaginable. On several occasions I went home in tears because of my disappointment and disillusionment. Notwithstanding these issues, I maintained a positive attitude about the ministry in front of my husband and family. I never wanted to deter my husband from attending with me, and I wanted my family to embrace this giant step forward I'd made.

My oldest brother was one of the first family members to accept my invitation to visit my church. However, the next day he came by our house and told me he didn't feel comfortable with me being a part of that ministry. "Why not?" I was confused and slightly offended by his comments. "Something there just isn't right," he offered. He advised me to leave the ministry. I thought and prayed about my brother's advice but decided against leaving. I just knew this church was right for me. I mean, the pastor sang the same song God had placed in my spirit.

A couple weeks later, my older sister visited the church and had the same sentiments as my brother. I was baffled. I didn't feel comfortable leaving; yet I couldn't understand why my family wouldn't embrace this ministry. At Bible study a few weeks later, the pastor shared a "word from the Lord" with me. She said, "Don't listen to anyone but Him. He's getting ready to separate you from anyone who doesn't believe because people are going to try and deter you from following Him."

The pastor's words soothed me. It was an answer to my prayer! Yes! I believed God was speaking through my pastor. A few days later, she called and told me to leave my family because they were going to become a hindrance to my walk with Christ. I listened to her, but once I hung up with her, I began screaming. Leave my family? Would God require that? Would God want me to leave my husband and separate myself from my family?

I prayed and cried for hours. All I could hear was

the hollow echo of my promise to God. "If You're real, I'll serve you for the rest of my life and I'll reject everything for You." I packed my stuff and my son, and I left. I left my husband and separated myself from my family based on the word of my pastor. I believed my pastor and this church was my doorway to destiny. In actuality, my obedience to the pastor and my zealousness for this ministry ushered me into one of the most devastating seasons of my life. I lost everything—my family, my marriage, my self-confidence and my self-esteem. I spiraled downward into a web of seclusion and depression.

Reflection

Cultivate your relationship with Christ
In retrospect, I realize that my initial introduction to Christianity was more about my relationship with a ministry than with Christ. I was looking for someone to trust in; and although I had the Bible, I made the mistake of believing the "word" from the Pastor more than the "Word" of God.

Kingdom Culture means trusting God
Popular culture depends on the customs and beliefs of the world's systems. When you depend on these standards for the decisions you make, your life will be open to chaos and confusion. Kingdom culture prioritizes your relationship with Christ. It is only through trusting and obeying the guidance of the Holy Spirit that you will gain clarity about God's direction for your life and the proper decisions you must make.

God's love covers and protects
As a child of God, you are covered by His love. God protects His children and no matter what deception, traps and stumbling blocks the enemy tries to launch against you, God's purpose will prevail. No attack of the enemy can succeed when you are operating in obedience to God.

Being confident of this very thing, he which has begun a good work in you, will perform it until the day of Jesus Christ.
-Philippians 1:6 (KJV)

A. List some experiences you've encountered in your pursuit of Christ?

_____
_____
_____
_____

B. Are you willing to surrender the world's culture for God's Kingdom culture? Describe some ways that demonstrate this decision.

_____
_____
_____
_____

C. Is your love for God based on who He is, or what He does? Please explain.

_____
_____
_____
_____

D. Do you believe that God has full control of your life? Why? Please explain.

_____
_____
_____
_____

E. How will you keep difficult circumstances and negative situations from separating you from your love for God?

_____
_____
_____
_____
_____

Chapter 2

Wolves in Sheep's Clothing

I walked out on my husband thinking that I was obeying God. I was utterly mistaken. In the book of Matthew, as Jesus is teaching about the Kingdom of God, he warns, "Beware of false prophets, which come to you in sheep's clothing, but inwardly they are ravening wolves" (Matt. 7:15, KJV).

I was a babe in Christ, naïve and unaware of the deception that Satan is so skilled at weaving into our lives. When my pastor told me to abandon my marriage, I did what I was told. I believed she was right, but she wasn't. One thing I now understand is that God never contradicts Himself. The Holy Spirit, the Bible and the Heavenly Father always stand in agreement. Anything else is a lie!

In hindsight, I know I should have sought the truth of the Bible, which states that "marriage is honorable in all" (Heb. 13:4). In fact, God thinks so highly of marriage that He instituted it as a holy union between man and woman back in the Garden of Eden (Gen. 2:18, 21-24). Not only does God esteem marriage, the Bible says He "hates" divorce (Mal. 2:16).

Believers must be careful to understand the enemy's plan as it relates to divorce. When you fall into the various demonic traps of arguing, infidelity and other situations, you are literally destroying a covenant that God ordained; and the effects on your life and your children are unfathomable. That's why we must become champions of marriage and victorious in our marriage relationships.

When my pastor told me to leave my marriage, I came home from work and informed my mother-in-law (who lived with us at the time), that Sheldon (my son) and I would be moving out and that she could stay. She was puzzled as to why I was leaving. My family couldn't understand it either. My oldest brother tried to convince me otherwise, but I was set on obeying my pastor.

In the wee hours of the morning, I gathered my belongings and my son. We went from a comfortable three-bedroom apartment to a home that we shared with two other families. I didn't let anyone know about my new location. My family didn't know where I was, and I agreed not to contact them.

> *"I was being manipulated by the pastor and didn't realize it. The can was taking another hit. Instead of being concerned and caring, as a pastor (shepherd), she was being accusatory and condemning."*

Out of obedience to the pastor, I abided by the restrictions of this new location. I made no contact with my family, so that I would not become "contaminated" (her words). This rule was extremely difficult to follow. I loved my family and I missed them. One day, I called one of my sisters and told her how much I missed the family; she pleaded with me to come and visit them, and I did.

My mother had always encouraged her children to stick together, and seeing my siblings brought back those thoughts to my mind. I knew I needed my family, but in my ignorance, I believed that they needed to come and join my church so that they could be with me. I reasoned that we'd all be happy if we were all part of my church.

That evening, as I arrived at the church, a torrential storm erupted. The downpour and explosive thunderclaps literally shook the house as we were having service. I was in the habit of taking my shoes off during the praise service to holy dance; but that night, as I was praising God, a sharp crash of thunder scared me so badly I jumped from my seat and somehow landed with the four-inch heel of my shoe stuck through my foot.

Blood gushed from my foot, but to my horror, no one came to help me. I couldn't believe it! I ended up driving myself to the hospital. The doctors said it was one of the worst foot injuries they'd seen and that I would need three months to heal.

As I writhed in pain, thoughts ran through my mind of the pastor's words during the service. She had admonished us that the storm was a response to God's displeasure with someone. I wondered if it was me, but I didn't have to wonder long. Later, when the pastor came to visit me, she pointed out that the reason for my severe injury was my disobedience in visiting my family. I was shocked by the fact that she had knowledge of my visit. I cried and cried, tears of pain mixed with remorse. I told God how sorry I was for my disobedience and promised Him never to do it again.

> *"Beware of false prophets, which come to you in sheep's clothing, but inwardly they are ravening wolves"* (Matt. 7:15, KJV).

I was being manipulated by the pastor and didn't realize it. The can was taking another hit. Instead of being concerned and caring, as a pastor (shepherd), she was being accusatory and condemning. The hurt I felt in my foot didn't compare to pain in my heart. I was made to believe that I had disappointed God as well as my pastor.

After my foot healed, I returned to the church, but things had changed. No longer were the members warm and welcoming, they had a different attitude. Their disdain was palpable. I felt like there may have been conversations about me between the pastor and members; conversations that showed me in a negative light. Amid all that was going on, my son took it upon himself to call one of my sisters and tell her about my injury. She called me and begged me to come back to the family. I'll never forget her warning me that something bad was going to happen if I didn't leave my church. I ignored her.

Between the injury, work, my son and the craziness at church, I had become exhausted. The trauma was taking its toll, but I was determined to be obedient to God and my pastor. February 5, 1994 was a turning point. That evening as I drove home from work, I had a strange feeling in my stomach. I didn't want to go to church that night. I was torn between my desire to obey and my gut telling me to flee from this situation. I had been at the ministry for three years and outside of my injury, had never missed a service, but that night, the thought of attending service disturbed me so much I could not disregard it.

When I got in the house, Sheldon presented a note from the principal. He'd been fighting at school and had received a two-day suspension. The queasy feeling in my stomach worsened as I realized that the pastor's reaction to Sheldon's suspension would be to send him away. She'd done it before and I knew she would do it again. I was in an all-out panic. I absolutely couldn't lose my son!

Despite most of the members' strange treatment of me, I still trusted a few women from my church enough to share my predicament. As I spoke with one of the women, she reminded me of the many families that had fallen apart after joining the ministry. Marriages had ended in divorce and children had been sent to live with other relatives. I couldn't bear the thought of losing my son. I decided I'd had enough. I packed up and Sheldon and I bolted.

When the other women who lived in the house came home and discovered that Sheldon and I were gone, they began a neighborhood search. However, one neighbor had become a friend and allowed us to hide in her home; she refused to answer the door when the women came searching. My house mates went so far as to slip a note under her door warning her that if we didn't return to the house, the devil would kill us all. Although I was literally shaking in fear, I couldn't go back. I resolved to leave the house and the ministry. I had come to a point where I recognized this ministry as a "wolf in sheep's clothing."

Reflection

Cultivate your Spiritual Discernment

Spiritual discernment is the ability to see things from God's viewpoint; to distinguish between right and wrong, truth and error. It is the quality of grasping and comprehending obscure concepts that are not evident to the ordinary mind. Spiritual discernment is essential for believers. Without it, we become vulnerable and susceptible to the attacks of the enemy. A believer cannot obtain spiritual discernment by reason or logic but must be acquired through knowing God.

If I had developed my spiritual discernment, I would have been able to see that this ministry was off track and I never would have joined or remained there.

To cultivate your spiritual discernment, you must cultivate your relationship with God. James 1:5 teaches us, *"If any of you lack wisdom, let him ask of God, that giveth to all men liberally, and upbraideth not; and it shall be given him."*

When you're in an intimate relationship with God, you will always seek his wisdom over and above the opinions of others. The power of discernment determines the quality of your life: such as who to marry, what people to choose as friends, when and where to move, and career moves.

> *"Beloved, believe not every spirit, but try the spirits whether they are of God: because many false prophets are gone out into the world." (1 John 4:1)*

"That we henceforth be no more children, tossed to and fro, and carried about with every wind of doctrine, by the sleight of men, and cunning craftiness, whereby they lie in wait to deceive" (Ephesians 4:14)

A. Write as statement that summarizes your understanding of spiritual discernment.

_____
_____
_____

B. How would you describe the importance of spiritual discernment in your life?

_____
_____
_____

C. Can you describe an incident or season in your life where you lacked spiritual discernment? How did that affect you?

_____
_____
_____
_____

D. How will you continue to sharpen your spiritual discernment?

_____
_____
_____
_____

Chapter 3

The Journey to Awareness

I finally broke ties with the ministry. I was free! Now what? The next season of my life was a difficult one. I had been so inundated with the lifestyle and rhetoric of the ministry, I was struggling with which way to go, and unsure of how to take the next steps. My life and mind had become so entangled with the messages of the ministry, that even though I was physically out, I was still mentally and emotionally bound.

Most Christians have never learned about cults and are woefully ignorant of identifying characteristics. It's important that Christians understand that many times unscrupulous people will use the name of God and even various scriptures to draw innocent victims in, and the results can be devastating. Jesus warns us in Matthew 24:11, "And many false prophets shall rise, and shall deceive many."

Cults operate both socially and spiritually. *Socially, a cult seeks to draw you in*. At first, there is an outpouring of love and support. When I first went to the ministry, everyone was wonderful. They embraced my son and me with open arms. There was nothing that they wouldn't do for us. They drew me in.

Cults seek to isolate you from your former life. When my

pastor insisted that I leave my ex-husband, I was initially appalled, but I had mistakenly viewed my pastor as the mouthpiece of God, so I obeyed her. The isolation from my husband was just the beginning; once I moved into the home with the other women from the ministry, I was forbidden to have contact with my family. I realized later that the women were keeping tabs on my activities.

Cult leaders twist the scriptures. The pastor often equated disobedience to her opinions and directives with disobedience to God. There were excessive warnings about the tragic results for anyone who disobeyed. This distortion of the scriptures was used to control everyone.

Cults manipulate the minds of followers. Being part of the group means abiding by the rules and regulations set by the leader. To rebel is tantamount to sin and can lead to separation or expulsion from the group. When I was injured and hospitalized, the pastor used my situation to manipulate my mind. Her utter disregard for my wellbeing was her way of manipulating me to subjugate my feelings—internally, externally, physically and emotionally, in favor of her dictates. When I returned to the ministry after my injury and my visit to my family, the harsh treatment I received from other members was a way to manipulate my mind and force me to conform.

Cults seek to manipulate reality. The leader and members of the cult promote an "us" versus "them" outlook that views everyone outside the cult as being against the cult's philosophies. Trusting and interacting with outsiders is discouraged. I had lost my individuality and had begun to view myself as a member of the ministry. Everything I did and everyone I trusted was part of the ministry. I barely interacted with anyone at work; the ministry had become my world.

When I was with the ministry, if anyone had identified it as a cult, I would have vehemently objected to that description. Ironically, I was totally unaware of the cultish aspects of this so-called "ministry" that were negatively impacting my life. The manipulation, control and isolation were apparent to my siblings, but not to me. Looking back, I thank God for deliverance, mercy and grace!

I had been in a cult for nearly four years and at the point that I left, Sheldon was my anchor. The strength of my love for him was the catalyst in my departure from the cult. There's something about the love that God gives us as mothers that is indescribable. It is that gift of love that saved my life.

After I left, it took me a while to detox my mind and spirit. I literally felt like I was losing my mind. There were days and weeks when I was depressed, and tears would roll down my face. I was in a season of chaos and confusion and although I knew I didn't want to ever return to the "ministry," I was frustrated because that life was all I knew.

> "...God brought me out of the cult with a testimony that would become a light in the lives of others."

My mental and spiritual healing came from rediscovering the truth of who God made me to be. It took time, but I began a process of constantly reaffirming the word of God about my life and purpose. I had to face the fact that although this "ministry," or more accurately, this "cult had damaged me" the reality of God's amazing grace still could prevail in my future.

After the cult, I felt beat down and devalued, so I spoke the words of Isaiah, "Because you are precious in my sight, and honored, and I love you..." (Isaiah 43:7, CSB). I had to remind myself that God sees me as a precious treasure that He loves and honors. He would never reject me, no matter what.

I felt broken and worthless, so I spoke the words of David. "I praise you because I am fearfully and wonderfully made; your works are wonderful, I know that full well" (Psalm 139:4, NIV). God made me in his image and likeness and he sees me as wonderful and awesome.

I felt powerless and pitiful, so I spoke the words of Paul. "For we are God's handiwork, created in Christ Jesus to do great works, which God prepared in advance for us to do" (Ephesians 2:10, NIV). No one could destroy my destiny. I repeatedly told myself that God brought me out of the cult with a testimony that would become a light in the lives of others.

The damage done by the cult could not take away the value inside me. Just like those dented cans in the Walmart, the green beans inside were still good and useful. I had to refuse to accept the labels that the enemy was trying to pin on me. It took months of prayer and meditation on the word of God, but God's truth always prevails.

I concluded that I was blessed in the city, blessed in the field, blessed going in and blessed coming out (Deut. 28:3-6). I was redeemed by the blood of the Lamb (1 Pet. 1:18-19). I was more than a conqueror through Christ (Rom. 8:37) and I was royalty (1 Pet. 2:9). Being aware of what I had been connected to helped me to deal with my feelings of depression. I had to make up my mind to stop focusing on my past and begin to focus on my future. According to Jeremiah 29:11 "For I know the thoughts that I think toward you, says the LORD, THOUGHTS OF PEACE AND NOT OF EVIL, TO GIVE YOU A

FUTURE AND A HOPE."
　I DECIDED TO LET GO OF THE PAST AND MOVE FORWARD.

Reflection

Ask yourself the hard questions

Asking yourself the question, "Who am I?" is the beginning of your journey to self-discovery. Unlocking the depths of your true potential, character and purpose is essential to being victorious over every trap that the enemy sets. What happened in your childhood? What significant events and experiences shaped your life? Perhaps your road has not been easy, but when you examine your past experiences and contemplate the lessons that you've learned, you will be the better for it.

God created you on purpose, for purpose

Understanding who God created you to be and what He created you to do is the foundation of your success. Romans 8:28 states, "And we know that all things work together for good to them that love God, to them who are the called according to his purpose." God causes all your experiences, both positive and negative, to work for your good and for his glory.

A. What are the most significant events and experiences of your past?

_____
_____
_____
_____

B. Describe how you've reacted in times of challenge and struggled. Have you ever experienced depression?

_____
_____
_____
_____

C. Write out key scriptures that encourage you and remind you of what God says about you.

_____
_____
_____
_____

Chapter 4

New Beginnings

It was time to start over. I had escaped the cult and now I was gaining back my emotional and spiritual strength. I settled in Los Angeles, found new employment and began attending a new church, Abundance of Christ Ministries. I reconnected with my family and my sisters gladly began attending the new church with Sheldon and me.

This new church was everything the cult was not. The pastor was nurturing but not in an intrusive or controlling way. The ministry encouraged healthy families and marriages and taught the word of God without any threatening overtones. I was thrilled to be asked to help with the youth ministry and took advantage of every opportunity to serve.

One of the upcoming activities that our ministry was planning was a youth explosion. I was excited to go around the community and pass out fliers and invite people to attend. One afternoon, my niece and I walked into one of our neighborhood businesses, New Life Gospel Record Store. It was a turning point.

As I was passing out the fliers, I noticed the presence of national Gospel recording artist, Dr. Norman Hutchins. He walked over to me and accepted a flier and then asked if the event was only for youth. I answered with a little extra sassiness, "Yes! The flier *says* YOUTH Explosion."

My response seemingly amused him, but he was obviously intrigued. I decided to push the envelope.

"Would you consider doing a free concert for our church?" I asked.

"Free?" he retorted. "Nothing is FREE! Can your church provide some type of honorarium?"

I was on a roll now. "No SIR!" I stated emphatically. By now, we were smiling hard during this exchange. "Sir???" He said, "I'm just as young as you are!"

"Where are you from," he inquired. "Belize." I responded and walked away.

At that point, I wasn't interested in connecting with a man. I was just 29 and getting my life back on track and providing for my son was my priority. The next time I saw Norman was at my church's youth explosion. He and I didn't speak at the event, but I became aware that he knew my pastor well because they had attended seminary together. A few months later, he attended another event at my church. This time, he approached me and asked for my phone number. Although it wasn't my custom to give a man my number just because he asked, I figured this was safe since he and my pastor were friends.

A few days later, he called and invited me to dinner. I didn't accept right away. I told him I needed to pray about it. I really wanted to be led by the Holy Spirit. After having been married and going through divorce, I wasn't anxious to be in another relationship. However, I prayed and felt a clearance from God. Three days later, I accepted Norman's dinner invitation. He took me to Red Lobster near Marina Del Rey. At the end of dinner, he handed me a little box, and to my surprise, inside was a diamond bracelet! My mind began racing!

First Thought: Is this an invitation to intimacy?

Second Thought: What price will I have to pay for accepting this bracelet?

Third Thought: He's not my type. It wouldn't be fair to accept his gift. I don't want to mislead him.

After leaving the restaurant, we went to the beach on the boardwalk of Santa Monica pier and played skee-ball. Then he took me home and made sure I got in the door before he walked away. And walk away he did, without even trying to go for a kiss or a hug! This was significant for me, because after being single for eight years, trusting and believing God, I did not want my flesh getting in the way.

When I got in the house I got on my knees and prayed. I asked God what I should do with this gift. Clear as day, I heard my mother's voice telling my sisters and me not to take anything of value from a man, because he may require something in return that you're not willing to give. I put the bracelet back in the box and resolved to return it to Norman the next day. I never followed through on that plan.

> *"I wanted someone who loved God more than they could ever love me; a man who would have no problem treating me respectfully and honorably like the gift that I was."*

Although I liked Norman, I recognized that the practicality of a serious relationship was far-fetched. He traveled the country extensively, preaching, teaching, and ministering the Gospel. I worked at the University of Southern California (USC) and served in ministry at my church, which I loved. Meanwhile, Norman kept calling, and even with my doubts, I kept answering.

    Despite his busy itinerary, he would touch bases with me while out of town, and upon his return, schedules permitting, we would meet for lunch or dinner. One evening, I decided to see a play that had just come to the Wiltern Theater in Los Angeles. I gathered my sister and niece to see "Is Silver & Gold Worth Your Soul," and guess who was in the cast? Yep, Norman Hutchins. We had not spoken in a while, so he had no idea I was there, but after the play my sister wanted to get her Playbill signed by the cast.

    The backstage line for signatures was long. When we finally got to the cast member area, I took the booklet from my sister to hand to each cast member for his or her signature. When we got to Norman, he blurted out my name in astonishment and then asked if he could take me out for coffee. I told him he could, but my sister and niece had to come as well. Ever the gentleman, he agreed, and we met at a Denny's close to my house. Once we arrived, he mentioned that he lived about 10 minutes away as well.

    After getting seated and ordering coffee I didn't waste any time informing Norman that I was not interested in a casual boyfriend or a one-night stand. I wanted someone who loved God more than they could ever love me; a man who would have no problem treating me respectfully and honorably like the gift that I was. To my delight, Norman assured me that he would do just that, and beginning that night, we were official.

    Once we were courting, I told Norman that if we were going to take the step of marriage, my father's approval was necessary. My mother passed when I was very young, so it was my father who raised and took care of all ten of us. He was a great man—a loving husband, father, leader and provider. The love he showed my mother demonstrated to me that marriage was a good thing. Even though their relationship was not perfect, they lived honorably and set a great example for us to follow.

I deeply loved and respected my father and I knew he loved me. He was protective of all his children, but especially his five daughters. I valued his opinion, and his approval of the man I planned to marry meant the world to me. I contacted him and told him about Norman and asked if we could get together so they could meet. In preparation, I made sure Norman was aware of the type of person my father was and the things he valued.

During the ride to our designated meeting place, I was so nervous I just began to pray. I wanted this meeting to go well and for Norman to meet my father's expectations. I was in love with Norman, but I hadn't told him yet. I wanted to wait until the timing was right.

When we arrived at the north campus of West Angeles Church, where Norman worked, Norman parked the car and came around to open my door. My father was already there, standing near the back gate of the church. When he saw Norman, they greeted each other like old friends. "Hey! Pop Garcia!" Norman said to my father, I was speechless! They already knew each other!

In Norman's capacity, as Director of Social Services for West A, he had often called on my father, a security guard, to assist him with rambunctious clients. Ironically, he never knew that "Pop Garcia" had children or made the connection between us. My father was well aware of Norman's ministry and had heard him preach many times.

Before I could ask any questions or make any assertions, my father looked at me solemnly. "This is a good man, take care of him!"

Take care of *him?* I was confused. As I replayed the words in my mind, my father repeated himself, confirming that my hearing wasn't failing me. Actually, it was a blessing to hear my father affirm that I was marrying the right man.

As far as I was concerned, we could have gotten married that day! Three months later we did marry, at the Justice of the Peace office in Norwalk, California. It wasn't my dream wedding, but I loved Norman so much, it didn't matter. Still, 18 years later, Norman made my dream wedding a reality. The ceremony was far beyond my wildest dreams!

Reflection

With God, starting over in life can be positive

Repositioning your life is never easy, but it can set you up for a better life if you follow God's leading. The key is prayer. Many times, when you're starting over after a breakup or a season of disappointments, you are tempted to be fearful and to over analyze even the smallest decisions. Yes, you should be careful, but more than being careful you must be prayerful!

Making the right moves mean aligning with God

God's word tells us God's will and way. When you pray and study the Word of God you will amplify your spiritual discernment. This is important, because gut feelings and emotions can be misleading. You always want God to be the guide in your decision-making. That means learning to trust him in the big things as well as the small ones. Remember, God never contradicts Himself (Holy Spirit) or His word (The Bible).

"For the Lord God is a sun and shield; The Lord bestows grace and glory, no good thing does He withhold from those who walk upright." (Psalm 84:11)

When considering a new beginning or opportunity, here are four considerations:

1. Is the new opportunity an answer to prayer? (Study Rom. 8:26)

_____
_____

2. Is the new opportunity in alignment with God's word?

   _____
   _____
   _____

3. Is the new opportunity a confirmation of God's promise to you? Does your spirit bear witness to this?

   _____
   _____
   _____

4. Is the new opportunity in alignment with God's way? If you have pushed, pulled or manipulated a situation, it's not God's way. God's blessings make rich and add no sorrow (Study Prov. 10:22).

   _____
   _____
   _____
   _____

Chapter 5

God's Mandated Assignment

Six months after Norman and I were married, we relocated to Dover, Delaware. The island-girl-turned-Californian in me was excited about the prospect of living near the beach. Norman and I had vacationed in Ocean City, MD and it was beautiful. Ocean City reminded me of beautiful Santa Monica (CA.). I thought Dover was going to be similar, unfortunately, that was far from reality. Our home was an hour and a half away from the water.

While I loved my husband, the East Coast was a foreign land with a different culture. Here I was, once again separated from my family. The next year and a half were challenging. I cried and cried. I felt like a fish out of water and missed my family terribly. I coped by looking at Dover as a temporary assignment that would soon end. I was anxious for the day that my husband would come home and tell me, "Honey, we're moving back West!" However, in lieu of hearing that news, I heard from God. One morning, during my devotion, the Holy Spirit ministered to me and said, "God didn't send you to Delaware for your pleasure, He sent you on a mandate."

I accepted the word of God that day and stopped my crying, but even though I dried my tears, my heart was still burdened. I didn't want to stay in Dover! I prayed to God to allow me to complete the mandate and release us to go back home. God did something better. He used my Dover experience to reshape and re-mold me for His Kingdom use.

To be honest, there were still some things in me that God had to shift. There were lessons that only God could teach me, and now He had removed distractions and crutches from my life. He was taking me to another level in Him and I didn't even recognize it.

In Jer. 18:2-6, the Bible tells the story of the Prophet Jeremiah being re-molded like clay in the hand of the Potter (God). Like Jeremiah, I was being re-molded by God for the future that only He knew.

God had positioned us in Dover, in a place called Kent County, which was not an affluent area. In fact, people there were struggling to stay above water financially. Understanding the needs of the people, we established Frontline Community Development Center. Our goal for Frontline was to provide financial assistance for electricity, food, gas, mortgage, transportation, and water for needy families. Two years later, Frontline Church was birthed, in order to minister to the "whole" man.

Working with the people of the community helped me reconnect my servant's heart with God's people; I joyfully assisted and served people from all races, cultures, and religions. But church was something entirely different. I had never been a first lady, and I was totally blindsided by the amount of scrutiny that came with the position. People critiqued me from head to toe and were quick to criticize me for anything they felt was out of order.

One incident occurred during a Sunday morning service.

I wore a gray St. John knit suit. The skirt fell below my knees and the top had a zipper that closed all the way to my neck if I chose to take it there. After my husband and I made announcements from the podium, I returned to my seat to find a text message from one of our church leaders requesting that I meet her in the restroom. Thinking it was an emergency, I immediately went to the restroom. She asked me if I was wearing a slip, stating that she could see through my skirt. I was stunned. I asked her to repeat what she said, and she did. I was humiliated and offended, but I reacted with grace.

One of our church mothers always carried a couple of different colored slips with her. I sent one of the ushers to ask if I could borrow one. The black slip brought to me was a size 14 and I was a size two, but I tucked and pinned it, so as not to escalate the situation, although I was severely impacted by the whole ordeal.

In our zeal to make sure that "church protocol" is in place, we often overstep and violate the "bonds of love" that the Bible prescribes (see John 13:34 and 15:12). Kindness counts, and hospitality should always be observed. If a person comes into the church dressed provocatively or in a way that is improper (according to standards of holiness), the church should recognize their opportunity to nurture that person's soul, to the point that Holy Spirit will direct that person to adjust their attire. Additionally, sometimes people who are unchurched don't have "church" clothes. People should be able to "come as they are" and be embraced without being forced to don lap scarves or endure scowls from members.

It was all coming together. My life in Dover was the set up for a great season of ministry. I was beginning to embrace my destiny and learn what God wanted to teach me.

I was being shaped into a servant leader. I had become adept at the servant part, but now God was going to train me to be a better leader.

As Norman and I sat down to lunch that afternoon after the "slip" incident, I shared with him what happened. He was outraged, but he asked me a question that made me think. He asked, "Karen, why did you let them treat you like that?" I didn't have an answer. I was the co-founder of the ministry and the wife of the pastor. Certainly, I deserved a place of honor and respectful treatment. However, I was still functioning through the lens of my past; I was operating with the residue of damage and dents. I had allowed the mistreatment and disrespect because I didn't recognize my value.

That afternoon, I shifted from damaged to destined. I made up my mind to no longer look at myself as "damaged goods" but to see myself as God sees me, as a daughter specifically designed and strategically positioned for destiny."

Reflection

Learn to recognize God's assignment

Recognizing God's assignment for your life will take place more readily if you are in a close relationship with Him. Distractions will cause delays, which is why God may choose to separate you from family, friends and acquaintances. But in that season of separation, your discernment will help you to see things from God's perspective instead of your own.

Learn to accept God's assignment

Recognizing and accepting God's assignment are two different things. Often, we want God's assignment to align with our own desires. Sometimes, people use the scripture found in Psalm 37:4 in error. They may say, "God will give me the desires of my heart," and suggest that God is like some sort of cosmic Santa Claus; but we often forget the entirety of the verse. The correct reading is "Delight yourself in the LORD, and He will give you the desires of your heart." Realize that this teaching of David emphasizes that the servant of God trusts in the Lord; seeks to do God's will in every aspect of his or her life, and trusts completely in the Lord.

As a result of trusting God and being faithful to Him, God not only directs our desires, He supplies them. Our "God" assignments are a blessing—to us and to others.

A. Has God ever separated you and put you in a desert (isolated) place? Describe this time in your life.

_____

_____
_____
_____

B. Have you experienced a season where God's assignment seemed to be totally opposite of what you dreamed about and hoped for? How did you respond?

_____
_____
_____

C. What challenging transitions in your life have led you to God assignments?

_____
_____
_____

D. Read Ephesians 2:10 – "For we are His workmanship, created in Christ Jesus to good works, which God has before ordained that we should walk in them." Describe how this scripture relates to your life.

_____
_____
_____
_____

Chapter 6

Destined by God

I finally grasped God's word mentally, spiritually and physically. My life changed when I understood that God had predestined me for His purpose and nothing and no one could destroy His plan for my life. Psalm 139:13-16 explains that God intricately and precisely wove each of us together in the womb. We were made for His use and His glory, and each one of us are special and unique, but we must be in relationship with God in order to find our ultimate fulfillment.

In the book of Genesis, the writer lays out the foundational design for all mankind. There, we learn that the same God that fashioned us from the dust of the ground is still the same all-powerful and all-knowing Creator. He has not lost control. He's still molding, shaping and guiding—even in the darkest times of our lives. God's ultimate purpose is to make you and I into a "masterpiece" fit for His use and purpose.

Once my perspective changed, I saw that every step on my journey was useful to God's ultimate purpose for my life. I started out confused, broken, misunderstood, and lonely. I had sustained damage at the hands of a cult, and a leader being used to destroy lives. But that wasn't my destiny; it was only my temporary situation.

My destiny as Karen Hutchins is to be a loving, caring, intelligent woman of prayer, faith, wisdom, and compassion. As I stand in God's strength, I disallow the opinions of anyone around me to overshadow the instructions of my Heavenly Father. My God-given mandate is to walk in my destiny as Vice President and Co-founder of Frontline Ministries, Chief Executive Administrator to Dr. Norman E. Hutchins, Founder and Director of Next Generation of Leaders, Chief Executive Officer of K Music Company, Bachelor of Biblical Studies, Doctor of Divinity and President of Daughters of Destiny Women's Ministry.

God was strategic in His chosen a path for my life; the struggles, misunderstandings, fights, heartaches and disappointments were strategic. But, because I didn't quit, I prevailed. My battleground gave way to my birthing place.

I never knew how to love past pain and trauma until I experienced the true essence of God's love toward me. I found out how to love people that mistreated me or didn't like me. I learned how to serve faithfully—whether or not I received a paycheck or a "thank you." I figured out how to rise above criticism, ridicule, blame and shame.

These lessons didn't come easily, but they made me who I am today. I discovered how to turn the other cheek when people honored and respected my husband but gave me the exact opposite treatment. I found out how to have true joy, and not depend on external experiences, situations or people to make me happy.

There were times in my past when I became frustrated with people because of my high expectations and their seeming disregard, but I learned to nurture others and avoid frustration, by speaking the truth in love.

I can say beyond a doubt, in the words of the old song, "If it had not been for the Lord on my side, where would I be." I would not and could not have survived any of this without God. These days, I live my life in a constant place of giving glory to God. He really is the best thing that has ever happened in my life.

My prayer is one of Thanksgiving:

Thank You Lord for not giving up on me. Jesus I'll never forget what You've done for me.... Jesus, I'll never forget how You set me free.... Jesus I'll never forget how You brought me out... Jesus I'll never forget, no never. And to show my gratitude, I'll tell others of your goodness, grace and mercy.

Chapter 7

Walking in Destiny

I know I am blessed to be a blessing. That means I fully acknowledge that my experiences, challenges and transitions were not just for me. I would never have become the leader I was destined to be if I had allowed the damage of my past to silence me. Many people feel ashamed of their past and only want others to see their "cleaned up" version.

I encourage you to take time to meditate on the purpose of God for your life. Your drama and trauma should not be wasted! Tell yourself that you are more than a conqueror. That means that no matter where you are right now, you are already destined to be a winner!

Here are some lessons I've learned that I want to share with you. Take time to meditate on these scriptures and write about how they apply to your specific situations. Perhaps you will write the next book that will help someone else recover from their pain.

In times of challenge, persevere and pray.
"Therefore, let us [with privilege] approach the throne of grace [that is, the throne of God's gracious favor] with confidence and without fear, so that we may receive mercy [for our failures] and fid [His amazing] grace to help in

time of need [an appropriate blessing, coming just at the right moment]." (Hebrews 4:16 AMP)

God will finish what he started.
"Being confident of this very thing, that he which has begun a good work in you will perform it until the day of Jesus Christ:" (Philippians 1:6 KJV)

God promises blessings for His children.
"Blessed shalt thou be in the city, and blessed shalt thou be in the field. Blessed shall be the fruit of thy body, and the fruit of thy ground, and the fruit of thy cattle, the increase of thy kine, and the flocks of thy sheep. Blessed shall be thy basket and thy store. Blessed shalt thou be when thou comest in, and blessed shalt thou be when thou goest out." (Deuteronomy 28:3-6 KJV)

Your salvation was bought with a price.
"For you know that it was not with perishable things such as silver or gold that you were redeemed from the empty way of life handed down to you from your ancestors, but with the precious blood of Christ, a lamb without blemish or defect." (1 Peter 1:18-19 NIV)

Spiritual discernment is vital.

"Dear friends, do not believe every spirit, but test the spirits to see whether they are from God, because many false prophets have gone out into the world." (1 John 4:1 NIV)

"But there were also false prophets among the people, just as there will be false teachers among you. They will secretly introduce destructive heresies, even denying the sovereign Lord who bought them – bringing swift destruction on themselves." (2 Peter 2:1 NIV)

"For false messiahs and false prophets will appear and perform great signs and wonders to deceive, if possible, even the elect." (Matthew 24:24 NIV)

"For such people are false apostles, deceitful workers, masquerading as apostles of Christ. And no wonder, for Satan himself masquerades as an angel of light. It is not surprising, then, if his servants also masquerade as servants of righteousness. Their end will be what their actions deserve." (2 Corinthians 11:13-15 NIV)

Salvation is characterized by positive change.

"You were taught, with regard to your former way of life, to put off your old self, which is being corrupted by its deceitful desires; to be made new in the attitude of your minds; and to put on the new self, created to be like God in true righteousness and holiness." (Ephesians 4:22-24 NIV)

"Do not lie to each other, since you have taken off your old self with its practices." (Colossians 3:9 NIV)

God loves you, no matter what others say about you.
"God pays no attention to what others say (or what you think) about you. He makes up His own mind." (Romans 2:11 MSG)

God is not a respecter of persons.
"So, Peter opened his mouth and said: 'Truly I understand that God shows no partiality," (Acts 10:34 ESV)

God's power and strength protects and empowers His children.
"His divine power has granted to us all things that pertain to life and godliness, though the knowledge of him who called us to (by) his own glory and excellence (virtue)," (2 Peter 1:3 ESV)

"What then shall we say to these things? If God is for us, who is against us?" (Romans 8:31 ASV)

God is in control, and we are like clay in His hands.

"Go down at once to the potter's house; there I will reveal my words to you." So, I went down to the potter's house, and there he was, working away at the wheel. But the jar that he was making from the clay became flawed in the potter's hand, so he made it into another jar, as it seemed right for him to do. The word of the Lord came to me: 'House of Israel, can I not treat you as this potter treats his clay?' – this is the LORD'S declaration. Just like clay in the potter's hand, so are you in my hand, house of Israel." (Jeremiah 18:2-6 CSB)

God was strategic and intentional in creating you.

"You made all the delicate, inner parts of my body and knit them together in my mother's womb. Thank you for making me so wonderfully complex! It is amazing to think about. Your workmanship is marvelous – and how well I know it. You were there while I was being formed in utter seclusion! You saw me before I was born and scheduled each day of my life before I began to breathe. Every day was recorded in your book!" (Psalms 139:13-16 TLB)

Acknowledgment

This is the LORD's doing, it is marvelous in our eyes (Psalm 118:23). I am tremendously blessed to have so many wonderful people who have been instrumental in the formation of who I am today.

To my parents, Maurice & Francisca Garcia, who continue to rest in eternal peace; there is not a day that goes by that I'm not thinking about you. You fostered a God-fearing daughter who loves God and is a faithful wife to her husband.

To my husband and pastor, Bishop Norman Hutchins, thank you for your support and encouragement. This book is possible because of your spiritual insight.

To my son, Sheldon, I am tremendously blessed and privileged to be your mother.

Special thanks to Dr. Teresa Hairston, Founder of Gospel Heritage Foundation, words cannot express my sincere gratitude for your wisdom, and meticulousness to details, to my editor Mikia, your hard work and expertise as an editor has brought this book to fruition. To Nicole Kinloch, my graphic designer, you are *simply the best.* Your creativity and passion for what you do is absolutely incredible.

Thank you: Susan, Cecil, Matthew, Fred, Ivan, Rose, Elsie, and Margaret for loving me and being the family, I can always call and depend on.

To my mentors, Dr. Tonya Lewis, Dr. Carrie Carter, Dr. Phyllis Brooks-Collins, Elect-Lady Brenda Bordeaux, Verna Porter and LaSheryl Hoyd. Thank you for your prayers and perpetual love.

To my photographer, Terrance Neal, thank you for capturing the happy, joyous and authentic me on the front and back cover. Kelly Halliday, my makeup artist, you outdid yourself.

To our Frontline Ministries Church Family of Dover, Delaware. You guys are amazing. Thank you for your love, prayers and support. Our love for you is incomparable. We pray God's continued blessings and favor to rest upon each of you.

To all my friends, thank you. It has been God who enabled me to transcend every obstacle and I am eternally grateful. I hope this book blesses you in a special way. I pray that you trust the Sovereign God whose power supersedes human ability, to turn what seems to be impossible to possible in your life. You don't have to remain "damaged," because of the shed blood of Jesus Christ, you can live victoriously and walk in your destiny!

www.ingramcontent.com/pod-product-compliance
Lightning Source LLC
Chambersburg PA
CBHW071414290426
44108CB00014B/1824